BRYCE CANYON
NATIONAL PARK

impact
PHOTO·GRAPHICS

Impact, 4961 Windplay Drive, El Dorado Hills, CA 95762

Photography provided by Bryce Canyon, Erwin & Peggy Bauer, Bob & Suzanne Clemenz, Ed Cooper, John P. George, Jeff Gnass, Dai Hirota, George H. H. Huey, Lisa & Mike Husar/Team Husar, Tom & Pat Leeson, Les David Manevitz, Joe McDonald, Lynn Gerig/Tom Stack & Associates, Kerrry Thalmann, Tom Till, Larry Ulrich, John Wagner, and Ron Warner

Illustration provided by Impact Photographics

ISBN: 1-60068-046-1

First Printing, February 2007

impact
PHOTO·GRAPHICS ®

4961 Windplay Drive, El Dorado Hills, CA 95762
www.impactphotographics.com

Printed in China

Nowhere else in the world have the ingredients of geology been mixed quite as they have at Bryce Canyon. Despite its name, Bryce Canyon has no great rivers running through it and is not even really a canyon, but a series of amphitheaters carved into the edge of a high plateau.

Fairyland Canyon, as seen from Fairyland Point, is a relatively small canyon packed with fanciful formations. Located between the park boundary and the entrance station, Fairyland is the first viewpoint inside the park.

Bryce Canyon gained National Monument status on June 8, 1923. On February 25, 1928 Bryce Canyon was officially designated as a National Park.

Appropriately named, Fairyland Canyon holds a myriad of fanciful forms. These hoodoos glow with golden hues in the rich light of morning.

Bryce Canyon is home to Black-tailed Jack Rabbits, Utah Black-tailed Prairie Dogs, the Yellow Bellied Marmot, and the Golden-manteled Ground Squirrel.

Sunrise Point is the first of four viewpoints which overlook the Bryce Amphitheater; though it is only one of many amphitheaters found along the rim.

The exposed tree roots of this young limber pine are graphic evidence that erosion is busily at work.

Thunderstorms, usually lasting approximately 30 minutes, are common in late summer at Bryce Canyon.

While the sun is emerging and illuminating the hoodoos after a thunderstorm, a rainbow stretches over the unique landscape creating a masterful sight.

In this view from Sunset Point, Boat Mesa can be seen beyond the Bryce Amphitheater. The top of Boat Mesa is protected by erosion-resistant conglomerate deposited above the softer Claron Formation.

Fresh snow blankets the Bryce Amphitheater. With elevations ranging from approximately 8,000 to over 9,000 feet, Bryce Canyon is cooler and receives more precipitation than neighboring Zion.

Thor's Hammer is one of the most photographed and well-known hoodoos in Bryce Canyon – located at Sunset Point down the Navajo Loop Trail.

Above the rim, where precipitation reaches approximately 20 inches per year and elevations range from 6,800 to 8,500 feet, the ponderosa pine forest thrives.

Hikers are dwarfed by the towering cliffs of Wall Street on the Navajo Loop Trail. As impressive as the views are from the rim, the true scale of erosion's work can only be sensed by taking a trail into the canyon and walking among the hoodoos.

Thor's Hammer rises above the hoodoos in Bryce Canyon. Erosion has carved the colorful limestone and sandstone formations into spires, fins, and arches, now referred to as hoodoos.

The natural orange and red hues that color the hoodoos are the result of iron oxidizing within the rock.
Bryce Canyon is truly one of the most spectacular scenic wonders in the world.

Sure-footed horses and mules take visitors into Bryce Canyon to get a closer view of the hoodoos.

Bryce Canyon Lodge, close to the rim of beautiful Bryce Canyon, has been completely renovated to its original rustic 1920's elegance and is on the National Historic Register.

In Bryce Canyon, the Claron limestone erodes in such a way as to resemble the crowns of royalty.
The hoodoos form through a complex process of differential erosion.

The high elevations of Bryce Canyon produce a variety of wildflowers, including Bronze Evening Primrose, Narrow Leaf Paintbrush, Head Cryptantha, and Mat Penstemon.

Fifteen miles across the amphitheater the Table Cliff's Plateau rises 2,000 feet higher than identical rock formations in the northern part of Bryce Canyon.

The narrow spire of the Sentinel stands among the hoodoos below Sunset Point. Rapid erosion of Bryce Canyon is often dramatic. Two-thirds of the Sentinel broke away in the early summer of 1986.

Inspiration Point sits at center stage of the Bryce Amphitheater. The canyons below the viewpoint are replete with magnificent art forms of wonders; it is the Silent City that steals the show.

This picturesque Wall of Windows along the Peek-a-boo Loop Trail is one of the most dramatic formations the process of weathering has produced at Bryce Canyon.

From the beauty of the Greenleaf Manzanita and Oregon Grape to the Dwarf Rabbitbrush and Bitterbrush, these shrubs show that form is also an essential element of the small scenes beneath our feet at Bryce Canyon.

Paria View overlooks a separate deep amphitheater carved into the plateau by the water of Yellow Creek. The forested floor of the canyon, more than 500 feet below, extends to the base of the cliffs.

From December to April deep snows can mantle the park. This season of lower visitation can be a serene period, perfect for cross-country skiing and snowshoeing. The view from Swamp Canyon is beautiful any time of the year.

Birds are one of nature's most beautiful creations, and some of the more common birds in Bryce Canyon are the Clark's Nutcracker, the Common Raven, Stellars Jay, and the Broad-tailed Hummingbird.

Natural arches are formed when rain and frost erosion carve an opening through a thin slab of rock.
When a stream carves through such a slab, the results are a natural bridge.

Agua Canyon viewpoint offers some of the finest lighting and color contrasts in Bryce Canyon and showcases the massive vertical cliffs that typify the rim along the southern portion of the Park.

A dusting of snow highlights the pinnacles of Agua Canyon. Snow patches commonly linger on shady, north-facing slopes until late in the spring.

Quaking Aspen commonly grow in the moist zones between forest and meadow. They have a cream-colored bark and heart-shaped leaves which become golden in fall.

Bryce Canyon National Park is home to several kinds of animals; you may even spot a few as you hike or drive. Mule Deer are common and can be seen regularly. Black Bear, Mountain Lions, and Coyotes are known to be in the area, but are seldom seen.

The Poodle is a hoodoo formation visible from Rainbow Point formed through the erosion of exposed Claron Formation – a blend of siltstone, sandstone and shale deposited as sediment around 50 million years ago.

The hoodoos of Bryce Canyon form through a complex process of differential erosion, organic weathering and frost-wedging. More than 200 freeze-thaw cycles occur each year, keeping weathering and erosion a dynamic force in shaping the scenery at Bryce Canyon.

From Yovimpa Point the plateau edges step down the Grand Staircase with views up to 200 miles.
Here, no higher forms impede the view into Arizona and sometimes even New Mexico. Visibility is best in winter.

The limits of life's endurance are reached near Yovimpa Point. Many Bristlecone Pines have died, while others barely embrace life through narrow strips of living bark on the sides of the trees. Bryce Canyon's oldest Bristlecone Pine has survived approximately 1,700 years.

Most visitors to Bryce Canyon get their first look at the region's colorful hoodoos while driving on Highway 12 Scenic Byway through Dixie National Forest. Iron oxides color the formations brilliant red.

As you drive through the Red Canyon tunnels, you pass through a gateway in time. During the summer of 1924, J.W. Humphrey, Forest Service Supervisor, was so amazed with the wonders of the area that he wanted to make it accessible by car. In 1925 Humphrey's vision became a reality when the Red Canyon tunnels were completed.

41

The towering red rock formations on the scenic drive along Utah Highway 12 through Red Canyon provide a beautiful contrast among the Ponderosa Pines. The areas away from the highway are usually quiet and empty.

Southeast of Cannonville below Bryce Canyon is an exquisite little state park. Kodachrome Basin was named in 1949 by an expedition of the National Geographic Society. The rich reds, oranges, browns, and grays of the oddly shaped Entrada, Henrieville, and Dakota, and Tropic formations are beautiful any time of year.

Shadows lengthen along the base of Grosvenor Arch, a rare double arch at the end of an isolated ridge of yellowish-white Henrieville sandstone, and one of the most photographed sites in the Grand Staircase-Escalante National Monument.

Another stop along Scenic Highway 12 is Lower Calf Creek Falls. This breath-taking desert waterfall plunges 130 feet over a sandstone cliff into an emerald basin below, and then slows along a course lined with beaver dams en route to meet the Escalante River.

Rounded by glaciers and colored by lichen, volcanic boulders dot the foreground while colorful aspen provide a backdrop to this scene along Scenic Highway 12 on the Boulder Mountain in Utah's Dixie National Forest.